What Does a Real Doctor Look Like?

Book 2 in the REAL Doctor series for Children

Dr. Cherice Roth

Fulton Books, Inc.
Meadville, PA

Published by Fulton Books 2021

ISBN 978-1-63860-498-3 (paperback)
ISBN 978-1-63860-499-0 (digital)

Printed in the United States of America

Thank you to all the people that helped me to see that I could be a REAL Doctor too.

Kaylon looked at herself in the mirror while getting ready for the day. Silently, she studied her reflection and thought, *I want to be a doctor, but I don't think that doctors look like me. Do they?*

She turned to her sister Kylee.

"Kylee? Do you think I look like a doctor?" Kaylon asked.

Kylee looked her sister up and down as she posed with her back straightened. Kylee finally shrugged and folded her arms. "Hmm…I don't know. I think we should ask Mom."

Both sisters rushed into the living room. Kaylon spoke first. "Mom, do I look like a doctor?"

Her mom turned from customer's hair she was working on and immediately said, "Of course, you do!"

The customer in her mom's chair lifted her head and spoke, "Kaylon, Kylee. Do you know what I do?"

The girls looked at the customer. "No…" both girls replied in unison.

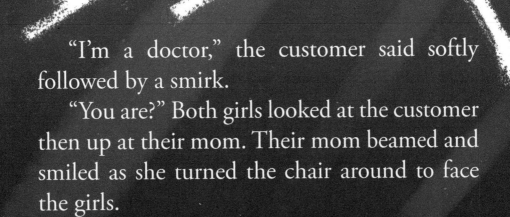

"I'm a doctor," the customer said softly followed by a smirk.

"You are?" Both girls looked at the customer then up at their mom. Their mom beamed and smiled as she turned the chair around to face the girls.

"This is my cousin and my best friend," their Mom said. "She is a doctor; she can answer all the questions you may have."

Both girls faced each other and began to speak too fast and loud for anyone to follow the conversation. The doctor held up a hand and said, "Hang on," and laughed. "Let me see if I can sort this out." She placed her hand on her chin and considered what she could hear from the girls.

"Girls, doctors can be men, women, and anywhere in between. They can be any color and ethnicity."

The girls looked at each other and sat down in front of the chair to listen.

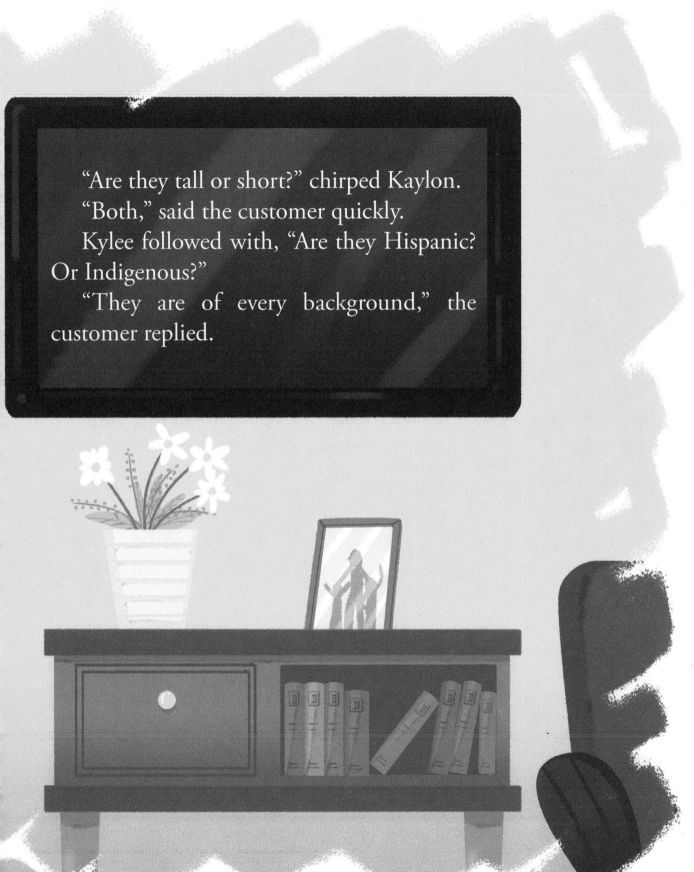

"Are they tall or short?" chirped Kaylon.

"Both," said the customer quickly.

Kylee followed with, "Are they Hispanic? Or Indigenous?"

"They are of every background," the customer replied.

Kaylon questioned, "Are they tall or short? Fat or thin?"

The doctor nodded and replied, "Yes and yes," then continued, "Kaylon, Kylee, doctors are not determined by their age, color, or any other physical trait for that matter. We are hard workers. Doctors are

moms, dads, sisters, brothers, daughters, sons, aunts, and uncles. We are all colors, orientation, differing abilities, shapes, and sizes! No two doctors are alike, but we are all hard workers, good students, and caring! So in a word…yes. A doctor can look just like you!" she said with a smile.

Kaylon and Kylee looked at each other then turned to their mom. "Then that's what we will both be," said Kylee grabbing her sister's hand. Both girls walked back to their bedroom each pausing to look at their reflection in the mirror.

With a smile and a lift of their chins, they stopped to enter their room; they both looked at each other and whispered… "Doctors look just like us!"

About the Author

Dr. Cherice Roth is a graduate of Texas A&M College of Veterinary Medicine. Before veterinary school, she earned a Master's Degree from the University of North Texas Health Science Center in Biochemistry. Before becoming a veterinarian, she was a college instructor. She spent time perfecting her exotic animal medicine and surgical knowledge in Australia and, upon returning to the US, mentored and guided veterinary assistants and DVMs in her home hospitals, while helping to develop and implement ongoing client education programs more broadly. She has held many roles within veterinary medicine from Texas A&M student ambassador up to Chief Veterinary Officer. Her most important roles are that of a mom and a wife. As a children's book author, she strives to highlight the power of representation in helping young minds to dream big! Outside of work, you can find her in the woods of Oregon with her many, many "Roth Ranch" animals, her sons (The Rothlings), and husband, or serving to help make veterinary care accessible for all critters.

CPSIA information can be obtained
at www.ICGtesting.com
Printed in the USA
LVHW072159051121
702556LV00004B/82